MW01592602

I Love You, But . . .

When a loved one has a problem with substance abuse

PATRICIA KRAMER

PREFACE

Substance abusers control all of the lives around them. Mothers and fathers worry constantly, rather than enjoying their lives fully. Husbands and wives live in fear for their relationships and the influence on their children. Sisters and brothers try constantly to give advice and support only to be disappointed and frustrated. Family members and friends become exhausted when they feel they have tried everything and failed repeatedly. The easiest solution would be to give up, but if we give up evil wins, and when evil gets a foot in the door it causes more pain and destruction than you could ever imagine.

*Never give up. Try every program and every idea. If that fails, try them again and constantly seek help. Along with the programs, look to God for the answers. One thing all family members and friends can do is pray for their loved one. The more prayers the better. Evil cannot exist in God's presence. Surround your loved one with the POWER OF PRAYER, and pray that God will guide you and them through this dysfunctional time. Pick a time of day and pray in unison that God would guide them to learn many positive lessons and evolve into a healthier, stronger, wiser, and more loving person. Reassure your loved one constantly that they are loved. They **need to know** they are loved.*

I Love You, But...

I want to be able to help.

Please God

Guide me,
because
as hard as I try
I can't seem to do or say
the right thing.

I Love You, But…

*When we talk,
I don't think you
hear me.*

Please God

*Open the lines
of communication.
Bring just the right
people to my loved one
to help them hear the
words they need to hear.
Please help them
want to get well
more than anything.*

I Love You, But...

*I miss
the old you.*

Please God

*Help me remember the
good times,
and I pray that You
would come to the rescue
and bring good health
and happiness
to this person we love.*

I Love You, But…

*We only do things
your way.*

Please God

*I give in so often
when I know
I shouldn't.
Please give me
strength and guidance.*

I Love You, But…

*I can't get through
your emotional armor.*

Please God

*Let them know
I am here for them
and sincerely want
to be close again.*

I Love You, But...

Sometimes you seem so hateful.

Please God

*Fill them with love
and kind words.
Please help them to
never feel hate again.*

I Love You, But…

*It's so disappointing
to learn that
you have lied.*

Please God

*Help me to sift out
the truth from the lies,
and
help them to recover
so they will never again
feel a need to lie.*

I Love You, But...

You're never around.

Please God

*It hurts
to feel so unimportant
when we used to be
so close.
Please help us.*

I Love You, But…

*You don't always do
what you say
you will do.*

Please God

*Help me pick up
the loose ends,
and help my loved one
to again
live with the feeling
of responsibility.*

I Love You, But…

*You don't even know
how you are
hurting people.*

Please God

*I know the hurting
is not intentional.
Help me to disregard
the painful words and
actions until You can
make my loved one
well again.*

I Love You, But…

*Your love seems
so conditional.*

Please God

*Help me to maintain
my deep and trusting love,
and help my loved one
realize
that substance abuse
robs them of the ability
to love unconditionally.*

I Love You, But…

*Some of the people
you choose
as friends don't
bring out
the best in you.*

Please God

So many outside influences have become so harmful. This special person deserves Your protection—please help.

I Love You, But…

*I wish you wouldn't
take advantage
of my weaknesses.*

Please God

I despise feeling
so helpless.
I pray for the strength
to say the right things
and do what
needs to be done.

I Love You, But…

*I feel like
you're
never satisfied.*

Please God

*Help me to keep
giving until
You can restore
their appreciation.*

I Love You, But...

Life is too short.

Please God

*We never know what
may happen
tomorrow, so please
help us not to lose
any more days.*

I Love You, But...

*You are so
out of control.*

Please God

*Restore their health
and cure their addiction.
Give me the strength
to be there for as long
as it takes.*

I Love You, But…

*I'm afraid
for our family.*

Please God

*Help our loved one
again feel the
responsibility of their
role in our family.
We need them.*

I Love You, But…

*You never
ask for my opinion
anymore.*

Please God

*Help me to live with
the disrespect
I'm feeling and please
show me signs
that You are
working on a solution.*

I Love You, But...

*You try to place
so much
blame on others.*

Please God

*The past can't
be changed.
Help my loved one
to know that we all
make mistakes
and that You are always
the first to forgive.*

I Love You, But...

*I wish you could see
that you are
in denial.*

Please God

*Help them realize
they have a problem
and then please give them
a miraculously easy
and speedy
lifelong recovery.*

I Love You, But…

*I miss dreaming
and laughing
with you.*

Please God

*Help me maintain my
sense of humor
and I pray that you
would return this
special person to me.*

I Love You, But…

*It hurts
watching you
destroy yourself.*

Please God

*It seems like it will
take a miracle
for my loved one
to pick up the pieces,
but I know
that is Your specialty.*

I Love You, But…

I'm afraid for your health.

Please God

*Give them the message
that this abusive
behavior is unhealthy.
I pray that
You will provide them
with the strength
and the desire
to recover.*

I Love You, But…

*I don't want
to lose you.*

Please God

*Help them to know
how precious
they are,
and help them to want
to be healthy again.*

Place picture here

This page is devoted to your own personal prayer.

Printed in the United States
36099LVS00004B/364

9 781597 813174